Mom Jokes

that put dad jokes to shame

Laughter is
an instant vacation.
                    Milton Berle

Mother: (n.) One person who does the work of 20 for free.

✼✼✼✼✼✼✼✼✼✼✼ ❀ ✼✼✼✼✼✼✼✼✼✼✼

What are the three quickest ways to spread a rumor?

The internet, telephone, and telling your mom.

I asked a police recruit during an exam, What would you do if you had to arrest your own mother?

He said Call for backup

✳✳✳✳✳✳✳✳✳✳✳✳ ❀ ✳✳✳✳✳✳✳✳✳✳✳✳

Why is a computer so smart?

Because it listens to its motherboard

✳✳✳✳✳✳✳✳✳✳✳✳ ❀ ✳✳✳✳✳✳✳✳✳✳✳✳

Daughter: Mom, I need my personal space!

Mom: You came out of my personal space

What do you call a small mom?

Minimum

✳✳✳✳✳✳✳✳✳✳✳✳ ✻ ✳✳✳✳✳✳✳✳✳✳✳✳

A mother said to her son, Look at that kid over there; he's not misbehaving.

The son replied: Maybe he has good parents then!

✳✳✳✳✳✳✳✳✳✳✳✳ ✻ ✳✳✳✳✳✳✳✳✳✳✳✳

Why don't mothers wear watches?

There's a clock on the stove

Why did the baby strawberry cry?

Because his mom was in a jam!

✳✳✳✳✳✳✳✳✳✳✳✳❀✳✳✳✳✳✳✳✳✳✳✳✳

What did Mommy spider say to Baby spider?

You spend too much time on the web

✳✳✳✳✳✳✳✳✳✳✳✳❀✳✳✳✳✳✳✳✳✳✳✳✳

What did the Mother broom say to the Baby broom?

It's time to go to sweep!

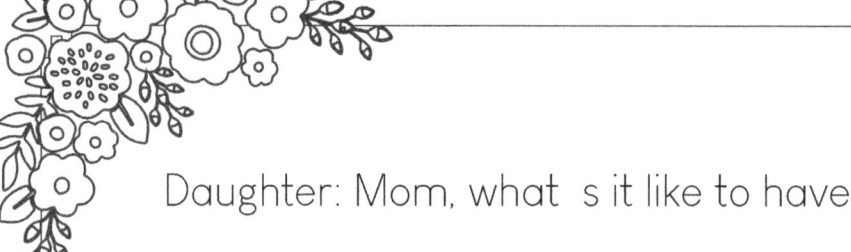

Daughter: Mom, what's it like to have the greatest daughter in the world?

Mother: I don't know dear, ask your grandmother.

************❋***********

Don't wake up mom! There are at least sevenspecies who eat their young Your mom may be one of them.

************❋***********

What did the panda give his mommy?

A bear hug.

What makes more noise than a child jumping on mommy's bed?

Two children jumping on mommy's bed!

***********✻***********

Why was it so hard for the pirate to call his mom?

Because she left the phone off the hook

***********✻***********

What sweets do astronaut moms like?

Mars bars

What was Cleopatra's favorite day of the year?

Mummy's day

***********✽***********

When your mother asks, Do you want a piece of advice? it is a mere formality. It doesn't matter if you answer yes or no. You're going to get it, anyway.

Erma Bombeck

***********✽***********

Nothing is really lost... until mom can't find it

There is a legend that if you take a shower and scream Mom three times, a nice lady appears with the towel you forgot.

✱✱✱✱✱✱✱✱✱✱✱✱❋✱✱✱✱✱✱✱✱✱✱✱✱

You know you're a mom when... ...picking up another human to smell their butt is not only normal but totally necessary

✱✱✱✱✱✱✱✱✱✱✱✱❋✱✱✱✱✱✱✱✱✱✱✱✱

Silence is golden. Unless you have kids, then silence is suspicious.

I don't want to sleep like a baby. I want to sleep like my husband.

✱✱✱✱✱✱✱✱✱✱✱✱ ✱✱✱✱✱✱✱✱✱✱✱✱

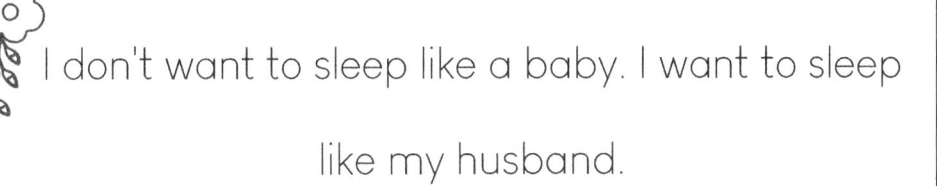

I hate when I'm waiting for mom to cook dinner, and then I remember I am the mom, and I have to cook dinner.

✱✱✱✱✱✱✱✱✱✱✱✱ ✱✱✱✱✱✱✱✱✱✱✱✱

Whoever wrote the song "Easy Like Sunday Morning" did not have kids.

What do you call a small mom?

Minimum

✳✳✳✳✳✳✳✳✳✳✳✳ ❋ ✳✳✳✳✳✳✳✳✳✳✳✳

A mother said to her son, Look at that kid over there; he's not misbehaving.

The son replied: Maybe he has good parents then!

✳✳✳✳✳✳✳✳✳✳✳✳ ❋ ✳✳✳✳✳✳✳✳✳✳✳✳

Why don't mothers wear watches?

There's a clock on the stove.

Logic: "If you fall off that swing and break your neck, you can't go to the store with me." Humor: When that lawn mower cuts off your toes, don't come...

✳✳✳✳✳✳✳✳✳✳✳ ❋ ✳✳✳✳✳✳✳✳✳✳✳

My Mom told me I'd never amount to anything because I procrastinate too much.

I said "Oh yeah? Just you wait"

I stubbed my toe and my Mom shouted at me for yelling, What the duck!

She was angry that I used fowl language

✳✳✳✳✳✳✳✳✳✳✳✳ ❀ ✳✳✳✳✳✳✳✳✳✳✳✳

What kind of flowers are best for Mother's Day?

Mums.

✳✳✳✳✳✳✳✳✳✳✳✳ ❀ ✳✳✳✳✳✳✳✳✳✳✳✳

Why did they have to rush the mommy rattlesnake to the doctor?

She bit her tongue!

Ah, babies. They're more than just adorable little creatures on whom you can blame your farts.

Tina Fey

Why did the mommy cat want to go bowling?

She was an alley cat

What color flowers do mama cats like to get?

Purrrrrrple flowers

What warm drink helps mom relax?

Calm-omile tea

How do you get the kids to be quiet?

Say mum's the word

How do you keep little cows quiet, so their mommy can sleep late?

Use the mooooote button

Why was the house so neat on Mother's Day?

Because Mom spent all day Saturday cleaning it

*************❋************

Why did the mommy horse want to race on a rainy day?

She was a mudder

*************❋************

Why did the bean children give their mom a sweater?

She was chili

My mom said she learned how to swim. Someone took her out in the lake and threw her off the boat. That's how she learned how to swim. I said, "Mom, they weren't trying to teach you how to swim."

Paula Poundstone

I love when the kids tell me they're bored. As if the lady standing in front of a sink full of dirty dishes is where you go to get ideas about how to have a good time.

My kids are never better friends than when it's 30 minutes past bedtime, and they won't stop giggling.

Remember when you first became a parent. And everything was so terrifying? Now you watch your kid lick the grocery cart and you don't even break a sweat.

✳✳✳✳✳✳✳✳✳✳✳✳ ✳✳✳✳✳✳✳✳✳✳✳✳

I let my kids follow their dreams, unless I already paid the registration fee on their last dream, then they follow that for six to eight more weeks.

✳✳✳✳✳✳✳✳✳✳✳✳ ✳✳✳✳✳✳✳✳✳✳✳✳

Children are like crazy, drunken small people in your house.

Is there any way to file a temporary restraining against a toddler? Just like 24 hours, maybe two days tops. Asking for a friend.

*********** ✻ ***********

When can we come see the baby? Four a.m. would be super helpful. Thanks.

*********** ✻ ***********

I want my children to have all the things I couldn't afford. Then I want to move in with them.

Delusions are often functional. A mother's opinions about her children's beauty, intelligence, goodness, et cetera ad nauseam, keep her from drowning them at birth.

My nickname is Mom. But my full name is Mom Mom Mom Mom Mom.

Pointed look from mom: "Give you money? Oh, honey, I already gave you life."

Motherhood is fun and all, but have you ever had the house alone on a Saturday?

✳✳✳✳✳✳✳✳✳✳✳✳✳❋✳✳✳✳✳✳✳✳✳✳✳✳✳

Bought my mom a mug that says, "Happy Mother's Day from the World's Worst Son."

I forgot to mail it, but I think she knows.

✳✳✳✳✳✳✳✳✳✳✳✳✳❋✳✳✳✳✳✳✳✳✳✳✳✳✳

Mothers with teenagers know why animals eat their young.

Why is Mother's Day before Father's Day?

So the kids can spend all their Christmas money on mom

✻✻✻✻✻✻✻✻✻✻✻✻❀✻✻✻✻✻✻✻✻✻✻✻

Son: Mom, what's a weekend?

Mom: I don't know, sweetheart. I haven't had one since you were born

✻✻✻✻✻✻✻✻✻✻✻✻❀✻✻✻✻✻✻✻✻✻✻✻

Boy: My mom is having a new baby.

Girl: What's wrong with the old one?

There are two amounts of pasta moms are good at cooking:

Not enough and enough for 3,000 people

✳✳✳✳✳✳✳✳✳✳✳✳❋✳✳✳✳✳✳✳✳✳✳✳✳

It's spicy, is universal mom code for I don't want to share.

✳✳✳✳✳✳✳✳✳✳✳✳❋✳✳✳✳✳✳✳✳✳✳✳✳

I love my kids.

Not enough to flip the fish sticks halfway through cooking, but I love them.

Mom's recipe for iced coffee:

Have kids.

Make coffee.

Forget you made coffee.

Put it in the microwave.

Forget you put it in the microwave.

Drink it cold.

Please excuse the mess; my kids are making

memories of me yelling at them

to clean up the mess

✳✳✳✳✳✳✳✳✳✳✳✳✿✳✳✳✳✳✳✳✳✳✳✳✳

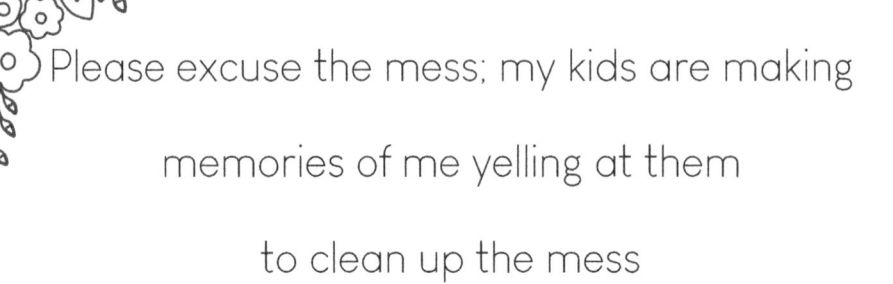

What do you call a mom who isn't around much and can't seem to get their underwear into the hamper?

Dad

✳✳✳✳✳✳✳✳✳✳✳✳✿✳✳✳✳✳✳✳✳✳✳✳✳

How many moms does it take to screw in a

lightbulb?

One, obviously, and she has to do it or else

it won't get done

Mom, are bugs good to eat?   asked the boy.

"Let's not talk about such things at the dinner table, son,"   his mother replied.

After dinner, the mother asked, "Now, baby, what did you want to ask me?"

"Oh, nothing," the boy said. "There was a bug in your soup, but now it's gone."

Baby snake: "Mommy, are we poisonous?"

Mommy snake: "Yes, son. Why?"

Baby snake: I just bit my tongue!

✽✽✽✽✽✽✽✽✽✽✽✽ ❋ ✽✽✽✽✽✽✽✽✽✽✽

To Mom: I'm hungry, I'm tired, I'm cold, I'm hot, can I have   where are you?

To Dad: Where's Mom?

✽✽✽✽✽✽✽✽✽✽✽✽ ❋ ✽✽✽✽✽✽✽✽✽✽✽

What kind of boat is barely staying afloat, yet somehow manages to function?

The mother ship

Mom: I have the perfect son.

Friend: Does he smoke?

Mom: No, he doesn't.

Friend: Does he drink whiskey?

Mom: No, he doesn't.

Friend: Does he ever come home late?

Mom: No, he doesn't.

Friend: I guess you really do have the perfect son. How old is he?

Mom: He will be six months old next Wednesday.

A kid asks his dad: "What s a man?"

The dad says: "A man is someone who is responsible and cares for their family."

The kid says; I hope one day I can be a man just like mom!

Mother to son: I'm warning you. If you fall out of that tree and break both your legs, don't come running to me!

Son: When is Mother's Day, Dad?

Dad: (wearily unplugging the vacuum) Every day son, every day

* * * * * * * * * * * * ✺ * * * * * * * * * * * *

What is a jumper?

Something you wear when your mother gets cold.

* * * * * * * * * * * * ✺ * * * * * * * * * * * *

"I'm homeschooling like that substitute teacher who rolls in the tv for a movie and just eats snacks in the back of the class.

My coworker at the hotel was miserable at his job and was desperately searching for a new one.

Why don't you work for your mother? I suggested.

He shook his head. I can't,

he said. Her company has a very strict policy against hiring relatives.

Who made up that ridiculous rule?

My mother.

My cousin was in love and wanted to introduce his bride-to-be to his hypercritical mother. But in order to get an unbiased opinion, he invited over three other female friends as well and didn't tell his mom which one he intended to marry.

After the four women left, he asked his mother, Can you guess which one I want to marry?

The one with short hair.
Yes! How d you know?

Because that's the one I didn t like.

Why doesn't your mother like me?
a woman asks her boyfriend. Don't take it
personally, he assures her. She's never
liked anyone I've dated.
I once dated someone exactly like her,
and that didn't work out at all.
What happened?
My father couldn't stand her.

✱✱✱✱✱✱✱✱✱✱✱✱✻✱✱✱✱✱✱✱✱✱✱✱✱

Fresh out of gift ideas, a man buys
his mother-in-law a large plot in
an expensive cemetery.
On her next birthday, he buys her nothing,
so she lets him have it.
What are you complaining about?
she fires back.

You still haven't used the present
I gave you last year.

A couple of hours into a visit with my
mother she noticed I hadn't lit up
a cigarette once. Are you trying to kick
the habit? No, I replied, I've got a cold and I
don't smoke when I'm not feeling well.
You know, she observed,
you'd probably live longer if you were
sick more often.

✳✳✳✳✳✳✳✳✳✳✳✳ ✳✳✳✳✳✳✳✳✳✳✳✳

Although I knew I had put on a few pounds,
I didn't consider myself overweight until the day
I decided to clean my refrigerator.
I sat on a chair in front of the appliance
and reached in to wipe the back wall.
While I was in this position, my teenage son
came into the kitchen.
Hi, Mom, he said. Whatcha doin ,
having lunch?
I started my diet that day.

When I arrived at school for my daughter's parent-teacher conference, the teacher seemed a bit flustered, especially when she started telling me that my little girl didn't always pay attention in class and was sometimes a little flighty.

For example, she'll do the wrong page in the workbook, the teacher explained, and I've even found her sitting at the wrong desk.

I don't understand, I replied defensively. Where could she have gotten that?

The teacher went on to reassure me that my daughter was still doing fine in school and was sweet and likable. Finally, after a pause, she added, By the way, Mrs. Gulbrandsen, our appointment was tomorrow.

I discussed peer pressure and cigarettes
with my 12-year-old daughter.
Having struggled for years to quit,
I described how I had started
smoking to be cool.
As I outlined the arguments kids might
make to tempt her to try it,
she stopped me mid-lecture, saying,
Hey, I'll just tell them my mom smokes.
How cool can it be?

✱✱✱✱✱✱✱✱✱✱✱✱✱ ✱✱✱✱✱✱✱✱✱✱✱✱✱

One rainy morning, my mother went for her
daily run. As she returned to the house,
she slipped and fell,
hitting her head on the driveway.
I called the paramedics.
When they arrived, they asked my mom
some questions to determine her coherency.
What is today?
inquired one man.
Without hesitation, Mom replied,
Trash day.

"They say women speak 20,000 words a day. I have a daughter who gets that done by breakfast."

✻✻✻✻✻✻✻✻✻✻✻✻ ✻✻✻✻✻✻✻✻✻✻✻✻

A toddler can do more in one unsupervised minute than most people can do in a day

✻✻✻✻✻✻✻✻✻✻✻✻ ✻✻✻✻✻✻✻✻✻✻✻✻

Some days I do yoga and don't yell at my kids. Some days I scream at them while eating cake over the kitchen sink. It's called balance

I love it when I find myself screaming 'STOP SCREAMING' at my kids

That's how i teach them irony

✳✳✳✳✳✳✳✳✳✳✳✳❀✳✳✳✳✳✳✳✳✳✳✳✳

One minute you are young and cool, maybe even a little dangerous, and the next you are reading Amazon reviews for birdseed

My mother is always trying to understand what motivates people, especially those in her family. One day she and my sister were talking about one relative's bad luck.

"Why do you suppose she changed jobs?" Mother asked my sister. "Maybe she has a subconscious desire not to succeed."

"Or maybe it just happened," said my sister, exasperated. "Do you know you analyze everything to death?"

Mother was silent for a moment.

"That's true," she said. "Why do you think I do that?"

The night we took our three young sons to an upscale restaurant for the first time, my husband ordered a bottle of wine. The server brought it over, began the ritual uncorking, and poured a small amount for me to taste.
My six-year-old piped up, "Mom usually drinks a lot more than that."

※※※※※※※※※※※※ ※※※※※※※※※※※※

My wife, a real estate agent, wrote an ad for a house she was listing. The house had a second-floor suite that could be accessed using a lift chair that slid along the staircase. Quickly describing this feature, she inadvertently made it sound even more attractive: "Mother-in-law suite comes with an electric chair."

While doing renovations in our house, one of the workmen paused to look at a flattering photo of me wearing makeup and a fancy gown. I heard him let out a low whistle and ask my son, Joshua, "Who's that?"

"That's my mom," Joshua answered.

"Wow," the man said, "my mother doesn't look like that."

"Yeah," my son said, "well, neither does mine."